The Oddball

The Years of George Putz, Jr.

by John J. Mutter, Jr.

ISBN: 978-0-9679770-5-8

another
fine,
print
by
Design
PottsinWisco@yahoo.com

Books by John J. Mutter, Jr.

To Slay a Giant
The Fight to Protect the Wolf River from the
Proposed Crandon Copper Mine.

Out in the Country
33 Stories About Nature
and Rural Living.

No Time to Count
The Life of a Small-Town Writer, (Author's
Autobiography).

I dedicate this book to the beautiful
people and Country of Ukraine.
Although your country lays in ruins;
the strong-willed people will rise
from the ashes . . . exactly
as did the Phoenix.

Someone once said, 'When a man or woman who has lived a long life and accumulated a vast amount of knowledge, dies, a library burns to the ground.' I feel that way about the death of a man I knew quite well, George Putz, Jr. I knew George since 1966, when we both worked at the Shawano Paper Mill together. He worked in the finishing department and I ran a re-winder.

Between the time I left the paper mill, in 1967, and when I retired from working for the State of Wisconsin, in 2001, George and I did not get together much, but we did communicate from time to time. After I retired, I got to know George much better, and I'd like to tell you what I learned about him. George had been a bachelor his entire life. Every so often I would call him and set up a time and would stop in to visit. Visiting with George was like this: two chairs about three feet apart, vis-a-vis, with just enough space for us amidst collections in the room, and we'd talk. I didn't know it at the time but George had a large safe in that room. He had created a space within the wall of the room and could remove a piece of paneling to get into the safe. The safe was about three feet tall, two and a half feet wide and about three feet deep. I found out about the safe after he died. Bill Maersch and I tried our best to get the place in order to dispose of all of George's possessions.

Let me start this out by piecing together George Putz, Jr's family tree. George's grandpa, on his father's side, Julius Putz, was born in Germany on April 25, 1865. He came to America at the age of six. He somehow met a lady by the name of Mary Degener, who lived in the Township of Belle Plaine, Shawano County, Wisconsin and they were married in Shawano by Justice of the Peace, Ed Sommers, on January 25, 1886.

Julius Putz had a brother Frank, who married Mathilda Degener, Mary Degener, Putz's sister. So two brothers married two sisters. Julius and Mary Putz resided on a farm near Buckbee, Wisconsin, which is Larrabee Township, Waupaca County, was named for J. E. Buckbee, a Union Colonel in the American Civil War. Buckbee is now (as of 2022), a ghost town. Frank and Mathilda Putz also had a farm near Buckbee. I think it's important to point out that Mary and Mathilda Degener's father, Fredrick Degener, Sr., was a Civil War Veteran.

Julius & Mary's Wedding photo, January 25, 1886

Civil War Veteran Fredrick Degener Sr., and his prayer card

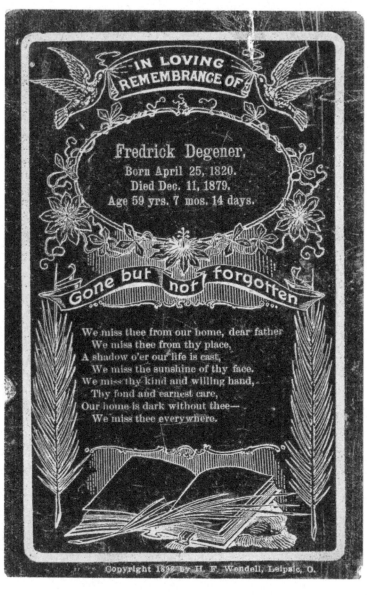

IN LOVING REMEMBRANCE OF

Fredrick Degener,
Born April 25, 1820.
Died Dec. 11, 1879.
Age 59 yrs. 7 mos. 14 days.

Gone but not forgotten

We miss thee from our home, dear father
We miss thee from thy place,
A shadow o'er our life is cast,
We miss the sunshine of thy face.
We miss thy kind and willing hand,
Thy fond and earnest care,
Our home is dark without thee—
We miss thee everywhere.

Copyright 1898 by H. F. Wendell, Leipsic, O.

Mary, George, Maybelle & Julius Putz Farm in Buckbee, WI Circa 1900

The Frank Putz Family at Buckbee, WI. Frank, Mathilda, William, Clara and Lily

The photo below is the one-room school in Buckbee, Wisconsin in which, among all the kids, Julius and Frank's kids are present. Maybelle Putz is the second from the right in the back row. George Putz is the fifth from the right in the front row. The teacher was Mamie Hamelton, far right in the back row.

The Buckbee area, WI, one-room school, circa 1901

On May 26, 1893, a wild fire went through the area and destroyed 24 buildings, including the Julius Putz home. In 1898, Julius Putz was employed at Bennets Broom Handle Factory in Buckbee, Wisconsin.

Bennets Broom Handle Factory in Buckbee, WI.
Circa – 1898 – Julius Putz on far left.

In 1905, Julius got a job at the Shawano Paper Mill and they moved to Shawano, Wisconsin to live.

The Julius & Mary Putz Family after they moved to Shawano, WI. In 1905, Maybelle & George in back

Julius and Mary Putz celebrated their 60th Wedding Anniversary on January 25, 1946.

60th Wedding Anniversary photo of Mary and Julius Putz

A little over a month after their 60th anniversary, Julius passed away, on March 1, 1946. He and Mary had lived at 304 S. Union Street, Shawano, Wisconsin for 39 years. Mary Degener Putz died on March 20, 1947.

Residence of Julius and Mary Putz for 39 years - 304 S. Union Street, Shawano, WI. Circa 1910

Julius and Mary's son George Henry Putz, was born on June 15, 1894, while they lived in Buckbee, Wisconsin. He was 11 years old when his parents moved to Shawano. He enlisted in the U.S. Navy on April 15, 1917. At the time he entered the Navy he was 5' 7" tall and weighed 142 pounds. He took his basic training at Great Lakes and during his enlistment he served on the Battleships: *USS Missouri, USS Pennsylvania* and the *USS Mississippi*, the latter launched at Newport News, Virginia on January 15, 1917.

He obtained the rank of Blacksmith 2nd Class and was discharged on October 8, 1919. After his Navy time, George Henry became a wanderer. His son George Jr., recalls stories of his dad going out west to look for work and working there for several years, in construction or in wheat field harvests.

George H. Putz while serving on the battleship USS Mississippi

George Henry Putz met Bertha Gross who lived in the Township of Hartland, Shawano County, Wisconsin. They married on January 25, 1923, exactly 37 years after his parents were wed. At the time, George was 28 years old and Bertha was 20. Bertha had a cute, somewhat mischievous smile on her face in most photos. They resided in Shawano at 814 Wescott Avenue.

Wedding photo of Mr. & Mrs. George H. Putz

George followed in his father's footsteps, working at the Shawano Paper Mill. Below is a 1957 Withholding Tax Statement from the Shawano Paper Mill, which might have been George Sr's last, as he would have been 63-years-old. He made $4,071.50 that year.

SHAWANO PAPER MILLS THE LITTLE RAPIDS PULP COMPANY GREEN BAY, WISCONSIN 39-0433835	WITHHOLDING TAX STATEMENT 1957 Federal Taxes Withheld From Wages
	Copy C- For Employee's Records
Type or print EMPLOYER'S Identification number, name, and address above.	NOTICE: If your wages were subject to Social Security taxes, but are not shown, your Social Security wages are
Type or print EMPLOYEE'S social security account no., name, and address below.	the same as wages shown under "INCOME TAX INFORMATION," but not more than $4,200.
393-03-2811 George Putz, Sr. 814 Wescott Avenue Shawano, Wisconsin	Keep this copy as part of your tax records.

SOCIAL SECURITY INFORMATION		INCOME TAX INFORMATION		State Tax Withheld
$ 4071.50	$ 91.64	$ 4071.50	$ 238.92	
Total F.I.C.A. Wages* paid in 1957	F.I.C.A. employee tax withheld, if any	Total Wages* paid in 1957	Federal Income Tax withheld, if any	

FORM W-2—U. S. Treasury Department, Internal Revenue Service   *Before payroll deductions
APP. I. R. S. 11-30-56

Income tax statement of George Putz Sr.'s, while working at the Shawano Paper Mill

George and Bertha

Bertha Putz & three month old George Jr.

George and Bertha had three children, George Jr., James Julius and Norma May. George H. Putz died on March 30, 1971. Bertha passed away on January 14, 1994.

George Putz Jr., was born in Shawano, Wisconsin on January 30, 1924.

George was born with what some people might call a defect—he saved most everything in his life. So, it's hard for a scribbler like me to piece the boxes and boxes of photos, letters and archival material, together, but I'm going to give it a sincere try, because George was a very interesting man, a friend of mine, and I think you should know about him. Some people might describe him as a pack rat, or a hoarder. George told me himself that he thought some people viewed him as an, "Oddball." Would you call a man who buys 133 dump truck loads of rubble from a demolished courthouse, and saved every canceled check he ever wrote, odd? That was George. George received his education in Shawano Schools. He took his studies seriously and got good grades.

During his summer vacations from school he was a self-proclaimed "River Rat." He spent a lot of time along the Shawano Lake Outlet, which flowed between Shawano Lake and the Wolf River. He was fascinated by boats and he also developed an interest in salvaging recyclable metals. He graduated from Shawano High School in 1942.

George Putz, Jr.,
at age seven

George Putz, Jr., High School Graduation photo

Number	Name Putz, George (Family Name) (Given Name)					School Year 194_1_ to 194_2_						Grade 12

PUPIL'S REPORT CARD

SUBJECT	First Semester						Second Semester						Credit
	1st	2nd	3rd	Av.	Ex.	Fin.	1st	2nd	3rd	Ex.	Av.	Fin.	
English 12	80	75	80	78		78	81	78	83		81	81	1
U. S. History.	80	84	80	82		82	84	82	90		85	85	1
Chemistry	80	81	91	85		86	90	90	90		90	90	1
Bus. Tr.	80	80	83	82		82							½
Relig. Educ.	90	90	90				90	80	85				
Salesmans.							79	81	85	78	78	78	½
Activities Gym					V4								V½
Times Tardy													
Half-Days Absent	2												

George's senior year grades

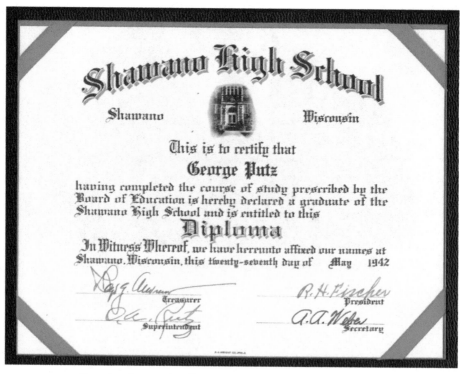

George Putz, Jr., Shawano High School Diploma

Sixty-second Annual Commencement

Shawano, Wisconsin

Wednesday, May 27, 1942

— Prelude —

American Anthem — Yeats ....High School Band
Mr. Harold Shlimovitz, Director

Processional ....Graduating Class

Invocation ....Father De Groot

Salutatory ....Bob Weber

Steal Away, Arranged by Hemmer ....High School Chorus
Mr. James Miracle, Director

Commencement Address ....Rev. Perry T. Jones

I Love Life, Mana-Zueca, Vocal Solo ....Mr. James Miracle

Valedictory ....Anna Brunner

Presentation of Scholarship and Loyal Leadership
Awards ....Mr. Reetz

Presentation of Diplomas ....Mr. A. A. Weber

Now the Day is Over ....High School Chorus

Benediction ....Father De Groot

*Program for the 1942 Shawano High
School graduation*

After high school George didn't waste any time being idle. Before the year was out George was employed at Iwen Box and Veneer Company in Shawano, where his father worked. World War II was raging, and George received an order to report for induction. The D.S.S. Form 150 letter read: "You will, therefore, report to the local board named above at: Courthouse, Shawano, Wisconsin at 12:00 noon on the 13th day of April 1943." At the bottom of the letter there were four paragraphs. One of them read: "Willful failure to report promptly to this local board at the hour and on the day named in this notice is a violation of the Selective Training and Service Act of 1940, as amended, and subjects the violator to fine and imprisonment." George was given a physical examination and deemed not fit for service. He was classified in Class – 2-A (F), and in one other document, 4-F. It was not specific as to why he was rejected, the only thing that was listed was that George had two toes growed (sic) together on each foot. Would that be grounds for rejection? Evidently so.

Then in 1943, both George Sr. & Jr., took employment at the Shawano Paper Mill. George Jr., ended up working 41 years at the mill, and he walked to work every morning, crossing the railroad bridge over the Wolf River, as he lived just across the river from the mill. He was a very dedicated employee, trying to do the best job he could for his employer. He worked the majority of his time at the mill in the finishing department. He operated the 131-inch duplex sheeter until January 30, 1970, when it was replaced and before it was sent off for scrap

The 1883 Shawano County Courthouse

iron, George removed the brass name plate from
the sheeter. The name plate read, "Built by Hamblet
Machine Co. No. 805 Lawrence, Mass."

In 1946, George bought property just across
the Wolf River and south from the paper mill for
$1,200. People he worked with at the paper mill
heard him talk about how he planned on building a
house on that land someday. George was infatuated
with history and architecture. When he heard that
the 1883 Shawano County Courthouse was going
to be demolished, he looked it over. It had locally
handmade red and white bricks on the outside.

In October of 1956 George contacted Madison Moving & Wrecking Company, who had the demolition contract, and made a deal with them. He paid them $230.00 to haul 133 dump truck loads (mainly the brick siding) of the courthouse rubble to his Wolf River property. Many people thought that George had lost it, as his property now looked like the aftermath of parts of Europe, post-World War II.

He began cleaning the unbroken bricks; the mortar and broken bricks were used for fill on the low-land part of the property. After around six years of cleaning the bricks, which were red, white and some yellow, he began spreading the word that he had some nice bricks from the old courthouse for sale. In an Acme Toplock Sectional Post Binder, George kept track of the bricks he sold. He started out selling them for .02 cents a brick. In 1963, he sold 3,030 of them for $68.50. In 1964, he sold 560 for $11.20. In 1965, he sold 14,485 for $287.50. In 1966, he sold 27,164 for $541.90. Then he held off selling them, and according to his Acme Binder, at 7:00 p.m. on June 11, 1968, he cleaned the last of the courthouse bricks, a twelve year project finished!

In 1970, he began selling bricks again, but had raised the price to .10 cents per brick. In 1970, he sold 231 bricks for $23.00. In 1972, he sold 4,860 bricks for $463.00. In 1973, he sold 800 for $80.00. In 1975, he sold 946 for $61.03. In 1976, 551 bricks for $55.10. In 1978, 130 for $13.00. In 1980, 100 for $10.00. In 1981, 16 for $1.60. 1982, 296 bricks for $29.00., and the last brick entry in the binder was in 1983, 385 bricks for $35.00.

133 dump truck loads of rubble from the 1883 Shawano County Courthouse

So was George Putz, Jr. an oddball? He ended up selling 53,554 bricks for $1,680.43. He would also use around 10,000 of the red bricks to side his house and one outbuilding. He had paid $230.00 for the brick rubble. Was it worth it? You'd have to look hard and far for someone to say yes to that. But George saw it as using something that was reusable. He didn't want to see it go to the Shawano Landfill. To him they were historic bricks and should be saved, not just in a neat pile in back of some garage, but used for siding on a building or to enhance a flower bed.

During the brick cleaning George came across a real keeper in his view. Before the handmade brick was fired, a cat had walked across it, leaving its paw print.

Cat paw print in one of the 1883 Courthouse bricks.
Photo by Wendy Johnson

*What was left of the 1890, Larson Brickyard, on Shawano
Paper Mill Property*

The Shawano Paper Mill property encompassed the remnants of the 1890 Larson Brickyard. George ventured to this site on many occasions and tried to salvage things from it. I think George felt nostalgic about this former business. Even though the buildings, were ready to collapse from years of lack of upkeep and weather, George saw some beauty in this dilapidated structure, and he wanted to preserve it, so he took a color photo, and had it enlarged.

George had a passion for art. The nineteenth century mansions of Wisconsin peaked his interest. Milwaukee was loaded with them and George would take at least one week of vacation every year and get on the train or bus to Milwaukee. He would always stay at the hotel he adored, the eight story, Plankinton House.

The Downtown Milwaukee Plankinton House, demolished in 1980

In the bathroom of his hotel room he noticed the ornate window glass and he copied it by taking a rubbing of it.

Rubbing that George Putz Jr made of a window glass in the Plankinton House

George found out that Marquette University had obtained ownership of a mansion and had plans to raze the building. George must have gotten into the mansion, as he knew there was a mahogany panel in one of the rooms, which he hoped to save. But the wrecking ball couldn't wait, and even though the mansion was demolished, George hoped that some of it had been saved.

Wrought Iron salvaged from one of the Milwaukee Mansions

He wrote a letter to Marquette University and this was their response:

MARQUETTE UNIVERSITY
OFFICE OF THE DIRECTOR OF PHYSICAL PLANT
MILWAUKEE 3, WISCONSIN

May 16, 1961

Dear Mr. Putz:

    We received your letter requesting the mahogany panel which was located in the building on North 14th and West Wells Street. This building was wrecked by the Modern Wrecking Company, 13925 West Lloyd, Milwaukee, Wisconsin, during the month of August, 1960, and I suggest you contact them directly concerning this item. Thank you for your interest in Marquette University and hope we can be of some help in the future.

                    Cordially yours,

                    Roy O. Kallenberger
                    Director of Physical Plant

Mr. George Putz, Jr.
Post Office Box 1
Shawano, Wisconsin

Response letter that George received from Marquette University

He kept a close eye on several Milwaukee mansions that were in jeopardy of demolition.

The Elizabeth Plankinton Mansion, built in 1888, bit the dust in 1980.

The Elizabeth Plankinton Mansion

George lost sleep over threats to demolish the 1892 Pabst Mansion, built for Captain Frederick Pabst, founder of Pabst Brewing Company. But in 1975, concerned citizens of Milwaukee got the building placed on the National Register of Historic Places and the public can now tour the 20,000 square foot mansion at 2000 W. Wisconsin Avenue, Milwaukee.

The 1893 Captain Frederick Pabst Mansion – Milwaukee

Dining Room of the Captain Fredrick Pabst Mansion

This is an undated hand-written piece that George wrote about the Pabst Mansion:

"I once had an opportunity to sit at a table in the Pabst Mansion kitchen and have coffee with the mansion curator while we had a discussion on old architecture. A large expanse of one kitchen wall was covered with blue and white, (individually scenic) tile. The curator had set up an appointment with me to view some photos which I had taken of the interior of the Elizabeth Plankinton Mansion (Demolished 1980) which stood just six blocks east of the Pabst Mansion. I had a tour of the entire Pabst Mansion, some areas which are not normally open to the public. Wisconsin Avenue in Milwaukee had almost 30 blocks of mansions at one time. Less than a half dozen are left. Milwaukee had a rich architectural heritage most of which has been leveled."

Early in his life George was interested in boats, as when he was salvaging recyclable things from the Shawano Lake Outlet. He had collected a few books on ships that sailed the Great Lakes. Maybe it was the fact that his father had been in the Navy, I'm sure that played a part in his interest in sailing vessels. In the February 1994 issue of the *Wisconsin Natural Resources Magazine* there was a story titled, "Seafaring Days" with photos of ships on the Great Lakes. It showed a photo of the *Milwaukee Clipper*, a Great Lakes Luxury Liner capable of ferrying 900 passengers and 120 automobiles the 85 miles across Lake Michigan from Milwaukee to Muskegon, Michigan. George had printed at the bottom of the page, "I crossed Lake Michigan about 40 times on

this ship." Why did he travel on the Clipper? I think it was just for the experience of being at sea, so to speak, and to meet people. In the boxes of George's possessions I found this that he had written to the historic preservation magazine:

"The picture and article about the *Milwaukee Clipper*, November/December issue 1990, renewed old memories as I made more than 20 round-trip crossings of Lake Michigan on the *Clipper*. One memory which stands out in my mind and heart is an incident which I witnessed about 35 years ago, this involved a man, a woman, and a pretty little girl about 7 years old with long blond hair. The girl was clad in a thin dress and the wind that day was cold, as it often is on Lake Michigan. The man and woman stood close to each other and were engaged in conversation, the little girl snuggled up to the man and said "Daddy I am cold" the woman reached down and pulled the little girl by her hair and arm's length away, the girl then stood there, silent, with tears flowing down her cheeks, the man paid no attention to her either. Was the woman the man's lady friend? Or the girl's stepmother? Whatever, she must have had a heart as icy as the wind that day."

"One pleasant memory is of an exhausted dove which came aboard about half way across the lake and stayed with us about a half hour, unafraid of all the people on deck, then when it was rested up, departed."

Going through the boxes of George's archival material I never knew what I would find that he thought was interesting or beautiful. I discovered this piece of letterhead paper that he had saved:

Ever since his teenaged days rambling along the Shawano Lake Outlet, George was interested in salvaging things. He regularly perused the Shawano dump and neighboring town dumps for recyclable items. He told me that he always had a hatchet in his trunk and if he found a discarded garden hose, he'd chop off the brass ends. In his Acme Toplock Sectional Post Binder, George recorded entries of recyclable metals that he sold. The first entry in this heavy recording document was on October 16, 1945, when he was 21 years old. On that date he sold 1,270 pounds of iron, but didn't list how much he received. From then on, starting with 1948, there are entries for iron, copper, brass, cast iron, aluminum, pewter, batteries, die cast, and zinc sold all the way up until August of 1970. There was even an entry in 1953 or 1954 for scrap paper, which he was paid $12.45. And then later in the binder I found more entries from 1980 up until 2002. There's a loose piece of paper with totals on from the first page of entries. According to George's figures, he sold 49,566 pounds of iron, 3,127 pounds of copper, 2,412 pounds of brass, 1,853 pounds of aluminum, 172 pounds of zinc and 389 pounds of die cast (as of August 1970). Income received from this first page of metals sold came to $1,280.26. On this first page of recyclable entries the most he was paid for aluminum was .09 cents per pound. On the second page of recyclables sold, he got as high as .70 cents a pound for aluminum, and that was on April 12, 1988.

On the second page of scrap metal sold, George began to fail in the recordings. The date and amount received was missing on one entry. But the entries went from 1980 to 2002. I'm sure there were more sales of recyclables, but he didn't get them recorded in the binder. The totals from page two were: Regular aluminum – 945.5 pounds, aluminum cans – 349, brass – 579, die cast – 36, #1 copper – 260 pounds, #2 copper – 1,306, and cast iron and steel – 3,980 pounds. Listed on this page, George even sold 28 pounds of aluminum foil. Income received from the second page sales was $1,559.26.

It's safe for me to say that George Putz, Jr., recycled more metals in his lifetime than anyone I have ever known, or heard of. He wasn't doing this totally for the money. He was saving recyclable metals from going to the local landfills forever.

I find the most interesting item George recycled was die cast. He would melt down pieces of die cast into rectangular bars on his wood stove. I wish I could have seen him do this. A picture of these bars are in an upcoming photo.

George never considered himself a rich man. But, when he had the chance to own a Rolls Royce car, he jumped at it. He bought the 1926 car and kept the registration for it. The license number was E7297 and the year was 1953. That's the only car he owned that he had a photo of. I don't know where he got it from or who he sold it to.

The only vehicle that George ever took a photo of, his 1926 Rolls Royce

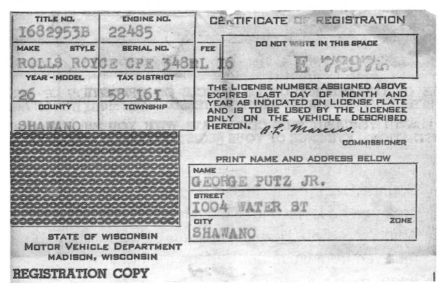

Registration of the 1926 Rolls Royce

Left to right, Kenneth Schwartz, George Putz, Jr., Don Stanek and Doris Anderson

George retired from the Shawano paper mill on June 20, 1984. A year before he retired the Mill Management gave him a clock, honoring him for 40 years with the Paper Mill.

During the early to mid-1980s, Wisconsin was embroiled in a controversy over a nuclear waste site possibly ending up in the Badger State at the Wolf River batholith. Targeted areas were mostly in northern Wisconsin, including parts of Shawano County. George saw this as a great danger to the area that he loved. He wrote a letter to Governor Anthony S. Earl. Here is the letter that George received from Governor Earl: on the right facing page.

State of Wisconsin
Office of the Governor

Anthony S. Earl

March 5, 1986

Mr. George Putz, Jr.
Post Office Box 1
Shawano, Wisconsin 54166

Dear Mr. Putz:

Thank you for your letter concerning a high-level radioactive waste site in Wisconsin.

As you know, the U.S. Department of Energy (DOE) recently named seven states as possible locations for high-level radioactive waste dumps and Wisconsin was among them. Two areas in Northern Wisconsin are under consideration as potential sites. One is the Wolf River Batholith. It is a 1000-square mile area that touches seven counties. The other is a 174-square mile area in the Chequamegon National Forest.

At this point the DOE will spend several years gathering data after which the president will choose a site. Construction may begin early in the Twenty-First Century. Under current law the Governor can veto a waste site decision but Congress can override the veto.

Although I feel Wisconsin has a responsibility to insure that nuclear waste generated in Wisconsin is stored safely, I am vehemently opposed to establishing a national nuclear waste dump in Wisconsin.

Wisconsin means "gathering of waters." We sit directly in the heart of the Great Lakes Basin, which contains the largest freshwater reservoir in the world. We have abundant groundwater resources. Our state also borders the Mississippi River and contains thousands of beautiful lakes and many miles of rivers and streams.

These water resources are interconnected, and even a minor waste leak anywhere in the Great Lakes Region would stand some chance of contaminating the world's largest freshwater supply for thousands of years.

Some argue that the nuclear waste "industry" might help the business climate. That argument is short-sighted at best. Any influx of federal jobs and money would be dwarfed by the catastrophic risks posed to Wisconsin's economic mainstays of agriculture, tourism, and even much of our present manufacturing base, which is largely dependent on our abundant fresh water supply.

State Capitol
P.O. Box 7863
Madison, WI 53707-7863
608-266-1212

I also place little stock in federal safety guarantees. Besides the fact that the technology is unproven, the DOE has proven difficult to work with, and its nuclear waste track record is less than reassuring.

Wisconsin will cooperate with the DOE's data-gathering. I am convinced that if the DOE makes a rational decision based on the facts, it will not sink tens of thousands of tons of nuclear waste into a site near the world's largest supply of fresh water. However, since I also have reservations about DOE's decision-making process, I fully intend to supplement their data collection efforts with our own scientific, geological, political and legal measures designed to make sure this thing doesn't get dumped on Wisconsin.

Wisconsin is already cooperating with Nevada in a court challenge to the federal siting process. We have established the Radioactive Waste Review Board to gather information and help direct citizen efforts. Information on the Board is enclosed and I urge you to contact the Board members.

In addition, Wisconsin's Division of State Energy is devising a plan to promote energy conservation and meet state conservation goals. Plans include the use of alternative energy sources such as municipal waste and renewable energy such as wood. There is also a very active program promoting the use of solar energy. Several hydroelectric generating sites which stopped operating in the 1950s are being reactivated and other sites are installing additional generating capacity. Finally, the Public Service Commission has declared a moratorium on building any new nuclear power plants.

Our decisions over the next 10-15 years will affect our descendants for 10,000 years or more. I hope Wisconsin citizens will prove to have the "staying power" required to maintain effective opposition to DOE's plans.

Thanks again for writing, and best wishes.

Sincerely,

Anthony S. Earl
GOVERNOR

kjs-8

Enclosure

In 1991, seven years after he retired from the Shawano Paper Mill he heard rumors that there was an interest in publishing a centennial book about the mill. Having worked 41 years at the mill, it was pretty much George's life. So he contacted the mill office and volunteered to research and write the book. His offer was greatly accepted. He painstakingly inched his way through 134 reels of newspaper microfilm at the Shawano City-County Library for research details of the mill. The results of George's work was the glossy 105 page book, *The Shawano Paper Mill Centennial 1894 – 1994*. Copyright 1994 by Little Rapids Corporation, and printed by Palmer Publications Inc. Amherst, Wisconsin.

When the book was released in 1994, George did not want any money for putting the book together. He got his reward when the book was released and all of the praises for the good job he did, and the many important people who attended the event, including Governor Tommy Thompson.

George Putz Jr., signing one of the paper mill books

George told me several times that he didn't consider himself a writer. I disagreed with him and pointed out that putting a book together as he did was not an easy task. A fair amount of text was his written words, not gleaned from newspaper clippings.

George always wanted me to attend the Shawano County Historical Society Meetings. So I tagged along with him to some of the meetings. The Society at that time was puttering along with not much direction. They were always looking for someone to be the new president. They kept looking at me because I was one of the youngest in attendance. In time I did become a life member and ended up on their Board of Directors, but my involvement only lasted around seven years.

After I had joined the Historical Society, I said to George, "Now, how about you joining the Shawano Area Writers group?" I guess he felt trapped, because I had followed him into the Historical Society, so he became a member and began to attend our monthly meetings. Many of the people in the group would read things that they had written, but George wasn't much into that. He would express some interesting things that he read or heard about instead.

I was the president of the Shawano Area Writers at the time and I worked out a deal with Rod Christensen, publisher of the *Shawano Leader* newspaper. The *Shawano Leader* would pay us $200 per quarter for material that we would send him for the "Accent" section of the *Shawano Leader*. So now I nudged George, who always said he wasn't a writer, to write something. I knew George could write because he had sent several Letter's to the Editor of the *Shawano Leader*, and then there was his historic paper mill book. George surprised everyone in the group when he wrote the following, which appeared in the September 26, 2004 issue of the *Leader*.

The Story of Grandma's Trunk
by George Putz, Jr.

My grandmother, Mary Degener Putz, was born in a log cabin in the Town of Belle Plaine, Wisconsin in the year 1862. At the early age of 12, she started working for Charles Larzlere at his boarding house/hotel at Langlade, in the north woods of Wisconsin.

When she had earned enough money, she bought her only possession, which still exists today, a Camelback trunk. The trunk was clad with sheet steel, bound with two-inch wide ash wood slats and was lined inside with printed paper which at the center of the trunk lid featured a portrait of a beautiful lady.

This trunk was undoubtedly purchased by my grandmother in Shawano and made at least one trip with her to Langlade and eventually back to Shawano by Stagecoach. Grandma spoke of going to Langlade with the Stagecoach.

Her job at Langlade must have offered few comforts. Her room was in the attic of the hotel and in the winter snow would blow in from under the eaves onto her bed.

An interesting little incident grandma told of was the time a man had kidnapped a bear cub and was running to the hotel with the cub under his arm, with mama bear in hot pursuit. Someone in the hotel seeing what was happening, opened the door just in time to let the man with the cub in and closed the door in ma bear's face.

Eventually grandma returned to Shawano to work as a maid in the Dayn Wescott home, which was located on Sawyer Street across from Lincoln Elementary School. Dayn Wescott was Wisconsin State Senator from 1893 to 1895. Grandma told that Mrs. Wescott had an aversion to seeing kids fighting and that she would cross the street to break up an altercation taking place in the school yard.

In 1886 grandma married Julius Putz and they established their home at Buckbee, in the Town of Larrabee. It was at this location that the trunk came perilously close to its demise. It was a very windy day on May 26, 1893, when fire raced from the nearby forest into the little community of Buckbee, destroying 24 buildings, 10 of which were homes, including the home of my grandparents. Grandpa and grandma had just enough time to carry a sewing machine and grandma's trunk to the safety of a field. By then the house was so engulfed in flames—there was nothing more they could save. They, and others sought refuge from the fire in a nearby tributary of the Pigeon River.

It was fortunate that the trunk was saved as it contained my grandparent's marriage certificate, wedding picture and a picture of grandpa's mother, also a group picture of grandpa's grandmother with six-year-old grandpa and his brothers and sisters.

After the embers had cooled, a scorched but unbroken teacup with a gold floral pattern on its side, still visible, was retrieved from the ashes of the home. This cup still exists today.

In 1905 when grandpa got a job at the paper mill they moved to Shawano with all of their possessions being brought to the city by rail car.

Their first home in Shawano was on East Green Bay Street, right where the Wisconsin Northern Railroad would soon establish their right-of-way. So they moved again to a house they bought on Union Street, where they lived until grandpa passed away in 1946 and grandma in 1947.

Grandma's trunk, along with other castoffs from the past, sat neglected and forlorn in the dusky loft of the garage where grandpa kept his model T Ford. After grandma died, my father was loading a two-wheel trailer with some of the accumulation of things from the loft which no longer had any apparent use, to haul to the city dump. Grandma's trunk would have went along had I not made a decision to keep it—could it have been a subliminal whisper from grandma, that made me keep it?

After 125 years the trunk looks a little tired. Though not rusty, its sheet steel skin has a patina of age and its paper lining is scuffed and tattered. I think though, it has earned a right to be cherished for its history.

I wrote this story from memory of memories related to me a long time ago by grandpa and grandma Putz.

The End

Note: This camelback trunk is now on display at the Shawano County Historical Society.

George surprised us again when he submitted a poem for the December 26, 2004 "Accent" section of the *Shawano Leader*.

Kitty Love
by George Putz, Jr.

A lonely homeless kitty
Is sitting by your door
Begging for a crumb to eat
Would you be compassionate?
To give her just a little treat
She once was loved and cared for
But now she has no home

For days she kept a lonely vigil
By her former humans door
Waiting cold and hungry
Plaintively she cried
I don't understand
My human doesn't care anymore
But kitty didn't know
Her loving human had died

With a passing of the days
Hope faded then was gone
Looking back once with sorrow
She walked out to the street
Knowing life would now be hard
A trial she would have to meet
Autos swerved, but not to miss
To hit was the cruel desire

Kitty mewed at many doors
Hoping for some help
She instead was harshly greeted
With brooms and sticks and stones
Oh how she longed to be inside

Those warm and cozy homes
Then you opened your friendly door
Kitty a haven at last had found

With timid pause she entered in
Never looking back
Then filled with food
And blessed with love
She curled up on your lap
Purring with contentment
Eyes closed in tranquil sleep
Sharing precious love
And companionship to keep
So long as you both shall live
The End

George was a cat lover. Late in life George lost his beloved, Tabby, who was 18-years-old. He took this very hard and later I will show some photos of Tabby. His love for cats is plain in the above poem. He also revealed the creative side of him by developing a fold-up 8 ½ x 11 inch piece of paper with a photo of a kitty on the front. When you unfold the piece of paper, it contained his poem—*Kitty Love*.

George had a humorous side and that came out in the July 10, 2005 issue of the *Shawano Leader* "Accent" section:

Instrumental Adventure
by George Putz, Jr.

Clarinet had a beautiful daughter, Viola, who was an impetuous young lady with an eye for men. From the time Viola was a little girl Clara tried to drum into her the importance of marrying a good man.

But the more Clara could harp about this, the more obstinate Viola became. Then, one day, as a freight train was slowly moving through town an oboe jumped from a boxcar and came to Clarinet's to beg for food. When Viola saw the oboe she told her mother, "I am going to marry that man."

Well Clara didn't like that at all and she fiddled around with every scheme she could think of to break up the romance, to no avail.

When the wedding took place the oboe gave Viola a wedding band which he had stolen. The wedding banquet was simple, just pork steak with strawberry cello for dessert. A few people tried to horn in on the wedding dinner. The oboe loved to trumpet around to everyone that he was an honest man, when in fact he was a thief and a lyre. He told Viola that he was a really rich man, but didn't own so much as a tuba toothpaste.

When cops came to pick up the oboe because he had broken into a phone company warehouse and stole one sack of copper wire scrap and two saxophones that was the end of the marriage.

Now free, Viola enrolled in a college course on archaeology, which led to her fame when she discovered a burial site for musical instruments and excavated the fires ever found Trombones.

The End

Our quarterly submissions to the "Accent" section of the *Shawano Leader* fell in December and this story that George wrote was on the first page of that December 18, 2005, *Shawano Leader*.

A Christmas Memory
by George Putz, Jr.

It was a cold, Christmas Eve. Twilight was turning to dusk and the manager of a Christmas tree lot was closing up for the season. There was one tree left. It was not a pretty tree, some of its branches were askew and there were places where nature had forgot to place branches. No one had given it a second look, even stragglers looking for a late in the day bargain had looked at it with disdain and walked away. The poor tree knew no one wanted it.

When it was cut and brought to the lot it had great anticipation of being part of a joyous Christmas for some family with little children. But as the lights of the lot were being extinguished one by one, the sad lonely tree lost all hope. Then out of the darkness came a man wearing a thin threadbare jacket, shivering from the cold. He told the lot manager, "I would like to buy that tree sir, but I don't have much money to spend. I lost my job several months ago and I have a little girl and boy and a wife to care for. There will be no presents this Christmas but that tree would bring some cheer to our home."

The lot manager looked at the shivering man for a moment then said, "Take the darned thing and go, nobody wants it."

"Thank you mister, this will make my little girl and boy so happy, have a blessed Christmas sir."

The children were so excited when daddy brought the tree into the house. They watched intently as daddy cut out limbs where there were too many and drilled holes in the trunk and placed limbs where they were needed, creating a tree as beautiful as any that had been on the lot. Even though there were no presents it was a joyous Christmas, filled with love for God and family and for a Christmas tree that no one had wanted.

The End

A note from the above author: This little story was developed from a lingering memory from many years ago of seeing on Christmas day one forlorn tree left where a Christmas tree lot had been.

At this juncture in the project, I want to convey the point, if you haven't already grasped it, that George Putz, Jr. was not only born with a love for the arts, he was an artist in many ways.

I'll take you back to the massive Acme Toplock Sectional Post Binder that I mentioned earlier. In this binder George had other things recorded. Some of it was poetry by others and there was one poem that was written by George, and it goes like this:

> The first time I saw her
> She was kneeling in prayer
> In meditation with God
> And the angels were there
> Hovering about her
> In candle light glow
> A lovely sweet flower
> Pure as new fallen snow

> The End

Sandwiched between the pages of the binder where the above poem was recorded, is a tearsheet from a magazine of one of Thomas Moran's best pictures, WESTERN LANDSCAPE. It was painted in 1864, during one of Moran's many trips to Yellowstone, Grand Canyon and Yosemite. Whenever and wherever George saw beauty, he tried to save it.

George's Aunt Mabel lived in Milwaukee. He occasionally wrote her a letter. He used the envelope as a place to do some artwork. Here's some examples of his envelope art:

GEORGE PUTS JR
SHAWANO WIS

SHAWANO. WIS
JUL 20
9 PM
1949

UNITED STATES POSTAGE
3 CENTS

CA BISHOP
822 SCOTT ST
MILWAUKE 4 WIS

SHAWANO. WIS
JUN 13
8-PM
1950

UNITED STATES POSTAGE
3 CENTS

CA BISHOP

822 Scott St

MILWAUKEE 4 WIS

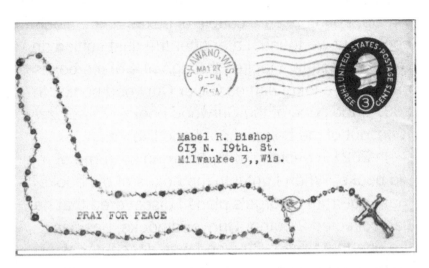

As I mentioned before, I helped to clean up and organize George's property after his death. There were boxes of old books, something I have a passion for. So, I purchased a couple of boxes of the older books that we found. Later after the dust settled on George's estate, I looked through one of the boxes and found a lot of James Oliver Curwood books. In 2007, I took one of the Curwood books, *The Grizzly King*, out of the box and read and liked it.

In 2021, I decided to try to organize some of my old books. When I got into the boxes of old books that I got from George's place I discovered that he had collected 21 other Curwood books, besides the one that I read. Curwood was described as an American action-adventure writer. His books were often based on adventures set in the Hudson Bay area, the Yukon or Alaska and usually ranked among the top 10 best sellers in the United States. I knew George pretty well, and these books just didn't seem to fit into his interests. What was the connection?

I went on the internet and researched Curwood. Earlier in this writing I mentioned that George had a passion for mansions. James Curwood had become very wealthy from his writing. At least 180 motion pictures have been based on or directly inspired by his novels or short stories. Curwood traveled abroad with his family and toured old European castles, and he was fascinated by them. Curwood came home to Owosso, Michigan and coordinated the building of his own 18th century style French Chateau by the Shiawassee River near downtown Owosso. The

James Oliver Curwood's Castle, Owosso, Michigan

castle wasn't built as a residence, but rather as his writing headquarters.

Somewhere George must have found a story about Curwood and the castle that he built in Michigan, which inspired him to start collecting Curwood's books.

As I said earlier, George loved cats. He got Tabby when she was just a kitten and she was 18-years-old when she died. To say that he loved Tabby might be an understatement. Like many families, they take photos of their children as they are growing up. George took many photos of Tabby in different poses. Tabby was a house cat and he never let her outside. When he was writing the Paper Mill Centennial Book, Tabby would be keeping him company while he toiled the hours away on the book. He would have notes spread out on his desk that he wanted to plug into the book at certain places. George told me that, "With one sweep of her tail, Tabby could set me back a bit, but I loved the little girl, and couldn't be mad at her."

Here are some of the photos George took of the feline that he loved.

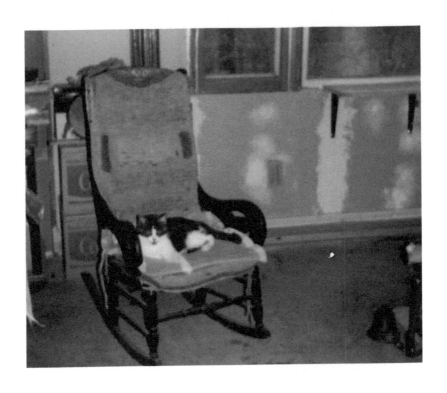

George was a religious man who in his early years struggled with his former church. In his late twenties he devoted many hours reading and researching the Catholic Church and on September 11, 1953, at the age of 29, he was baptized and made his first confession in the Catholic faith. But he didn't always agree with some of the moves the Catholic Church made, such as Vatican II, but he still attended Sunday Mass regularly.

George was adamant about protecting the unborn and would sign any petition that was opposed to abortion. For about the last decade of his life he printed, in red ink on his personal checks – "God loves the child in the womb too!" He also printed "AD" to the left of the date, which in Latin is Anno Domini, which means, "In the Year of the Lord."

GEORGE PUTZ, JR.
P. O. BOX 1
SHAWANO, WI 54166

79-1088/759 18
0032060185

1669

AD   DATE 01-12-04

PAY TO THE ORDER OF Catholic Diocese of Green Bay/BA $ 100.00

ONE Hundred and No/00 ~~~~~~~~~ DOLLARS

God Loves the Child In the Womb Too.

M&I Bank of Shawano
Shawano, Wisconsin 54166

MEMO _____

George Putz

⑆075910882⑆ 003 20⑈60 165⑈ 1669   ⑇00000 10000⑇

George was a law abiding man, without even a traffic citation. He kept his distance from those who had trouble with or took on the law. In the late 1990s, when the Crandon mine issue was tearing the State of Wisconsin apart, George believed those opposed to the mine were wasting their time, and felt the mining companies and their billions of dollars would win out in the end. George was wrong on that one.

As you walked into George's house, his kitchen was on the right, with a door to the garage. Straight ahead was what was to be a living room, which never was finished. Just before the living room, to the left, was a hallway with a spare bedroom on the right. Across the hall was the bathroom and just beyond the bathroom was a small room that he had designed to be his chapel.

There was a place to kneel, and some narrow shelves arranged for candles, religious statues, and various icons. There was one window in this small room, which was a stained glass portrait of Jesus holding a lamb that George had bought from a church that was either being razed or remodeled.

George never finished the chapel, but what work he did was excellent craftsmanship.

Stained Glass Portrait of Jesus

Photo by Wendy Johnson

Above is a photo of some of the oddest items that were found in George's house.

1.) Two packages of 50 clothes pins. One made by Forester Mfg. Company, Wilton, Maine, with a price tag on it for $1.49. The second made by Penley Corporation, West Paris, Maine.

2.) A rolled up, 43" long panoramic photo of the Battleship, *USS Mississippi BB-41*. George's father, George Sr., served on this ship during WWI.

3.) The Acme Top lock Sectional Post Binder that George kept his records in. Its 12¾ x 10".

4.) Centers of plates that George saw some beauty in. He somehow chipped out the center of two different sizes. There were five – 4" dia. and 13 – 3" dia. and one 8" dia. The plates are "Creative Royal Elegance Fine China of Japan." I have no idea what George had planned for these. Maybe chipped and deemed worthless, George wanted to save some of their beauty.

5.) Brown glass bottle bottoms that George had somehow cut. There are 18 pieces 2⅞ x 1⅛". Then there are 33—2½" in dia.

6.) Looks to be the start of a beer bottle cap collection. Guinness Draught, Cerveza Monterrey, Tsingtao, Cerveza Monterrey Light, Stevens Point Brewery, Beck's, Leinies Oktoberfest, Rock Green Light, Rolling Rock, Michelob Light, Milwaukee's Best, and two caps without a name, but different.

7.) A half full jar of brass zipper teeth. George told me that it was a tedious job collecting them.

I think I know what some people might be thinking at this point, "Why?" I believe that it was drilled into George's mind that, "Idle hands were tools of the devil," and George tried to stay busy doing things, even boring things, like collecting brass zipper teeth.

8.) A brass plate, which is from the 131-inch duplex sheeter that George worked on until it was scrapped in 1970.

9.) A small box of Manufacturer's nameplates that George collected, and neatly wrapped in paper so they wouldn't get scratched up.

10.) On the back of this brass door knob plate he'd found George had written on a piece of paper, "From 404 S. Lincoln St. Shawano, WI. Demolished March 1987. Salvaged by George Putz, Jr."

11.) Two bars of melted down material from TV sets. The biggest piece on the left weighs 8 lbs and stamped on it is: "TV Face Frame" The smaller one weighs 2½ lbs and stamped on it is: "TV die cast." I don't know how George melted this die cast material down, all I saw in his workshop was a wood burning space heater.

George had a table saw, jig saw, a wood lathe and numerous hand tools. He was interested in woodworking. Below is some woodworking and inlay work that he accomplished:

*Wood working at the entryway
to his unfinished living room*

Just before the millennium a landmark in his own backyard came tumbling down. It had been talked about for many months and then the old Shawano High School, 210 South Franklin Street, was razed. George received permission to look the school over before it was demolished. He had someone take a photo of him inside the school the day he walked through the rooms and hallways for the last time.

Shawano High School

George inside the old Shawano High School for the last time

Time to say goodbye to landmark

To the editor:

The time has come to say goodbye to a Shawano landmark. With a feeling of sorrow, tinged with nostalgia, we watch the walls of Franklin Middle School being reduced to rubble. The demise of this venerable old building, which orginally was Shawano High, will not only leave an expanse of vacant land near downtown Shawano, it will leave a void in the hearts of many who, as students or teachers, spent a part of their lives in this monument of classic architecture. A wreaking ball can destroy the building but only the passing of time will erase memories associated with it.

This past November, I had an opportunity to visit "Old Shawano High" for what would be the last time. As I reflectively walked through the building I found that the 55 years since graduating from there had diminished my memory of in which of its many rooms I had attended classes. The stroll did rekindle some memories that had long been dormant, of people and events associated with my four years there as a student. There were changes evident, The inclined floor of the once spacious auditorium had been made level and the area divided into several rooms.

Only a trace remained of its beautiful stage from which in 1939 renowned poet and author Carl Sandburg gave a presentation of some of his poetry and stories for the student body, including some of his as yet unpublished works. Another big change to the building was a hodgepodge of additions which closed off many windows, making the once bright and

cheery interior a drab and gloomy place; and no less so the gymnasium, where in 1940 tennis star and Wimbledon champion, Bobby Riggs, met with members of the Shawano High tennis

team, giving them some valuable pointers on the game. Two alumnus Shawano high tennis players, Merle Cooper and Jim Larson, came back to school that day to meet Bobby and had an opportunity to volley with him in the gym. Shawano High tennis teams took state championships in 1939, 1940 and 1941. The first year that state tennis matches were held was 1939.

Shawano never had an abundance of significant architecture making it regrettable that we had to lose this gem. The two west entrances of the building were embellished with architectural art seldom seen on buildings built today, sculptural stonework. Along with the generous quantity of stone accent where open books or stone set in the brick on each side of the two doorways. The entrance structures also had quoins, which are alternating long and short blocks of stone set in the brick at the corner of a wall. The hospital is the only other building in Shawano that I know of that has quoins. All of the stonework of the Franklin School was white, to contrast its red brick.

In the Shawano high yearbook (Shawnee) of 1942, there is a picture that was taken from inside the building at the southwest entry. Standing on the steps at the open doors, looking back into the building and waving goodbye are officers of the class of '42. Beneath the picture is this caption: Senior officers, Dick Rosenberg, president; Bill Dicky, vice president; and Mildred

Cowan, secretary-treasurer; bid you HAIL AND FAREWELL. From paragraphs alongside the picture are taken these words: "Just as all music, an end draws near — the strains produced in this school will stay in the minds of all concerned for a long time." A fitting epitaph for old Shawano High.

George Putz Jr.
Class of '42

George had begun to develop a logo at the end of his work, see it at bottom right of the above artwork.

Being of the Catholic Faith, and even though the Church changed some long and hard beliefs, George continued to avoid meat on Fridays. For many years he drove to a Pella, Wisconsin bar and had a fish fry and a bottle of beer at Hurricane Dawns. Fish was served starting at 4:00 p.m. and George would get there around 3:50 p.m. He would turn left at the tavern, go down the street and turn around. Then he would park just in front of the stop sign, ready to leave for home after his meal. This was a ritual of his and I won't even guess at how many times over the years he did this. I had the pleasure of joining him there one time for a fish fry, (and . . . one bottle of beer was his limit).

I have only scratched the surface of George Putz's life. One time during our face to face conversations George told me that he had suffered a stroke. He was affected on one side of his body.

But he didn't go to the doctor, and according to him he recovered. That was several years before he passed.

I know as the author of a book such as this, I have a responsibility of revealing my thoughts about George Putz, Jr's life, to solidify your inklings and questions. I'll do my best.

George loved Shawano, Wisconsin. He loved the Shawano Paper Mill, a three-generation strong love. A company that never ran out of work, nor money— money to clothe, feed and build security in his family tree and his community.

He loved architecture and battled to save it wherever it was threatened of being wiped off the face of the earth. He grieved over the loss of it; it was personal to him.

In our face-to-face discussions literally three-feet-apart, he shared with me that he felt the world was lost, and it was a waste of time trying to save it. I disagreed. In his eyes mankind had gone amiss. At times I felt as though I was talking to a misanthrope. He was mad at the world for allowing babies in the womb to be murdered. As he aged I hated to watch him become engulfed in a negative world.

For the last decade and a half, George could be found at the Shawano flea market every Sunday morning, hunting for forgotten artifacts and treasures of the past and talking with older people about things of years ago. I have the gut feeling that George carried an above average IQ with him. Many people thought he had a college degree—that's what absorbing the words of many books will do to a person.

Thinking back to our last visit George told me, "After I'm gone they will crash, smash this place of mine". I disagreed. But I was wrong on that one. Soon after the City of Shawano got ownership of his property, George's house, that was built on blocks, had a two-year-old asphalt roof, and could have been easily moved, was razed. The 10,000 salvaged and cleaned bricks from the 1883 Shawano County Courthouse that sided the house ended up where he didn't want them to go—the Shawano landfill.

Even though George's house (pictured above) is now gone, it can never be forgotten as postcards showing his house and property still exist. (Postcard photo below by Guy A. Wyman)

Greetings from Shawano, Wisconsin

George's Home

Shawano Paper Mill

After all of George's earthly possessions were sold, only one-third of his estate remained in Shawano. Thanks to his Uncle Elmer Gross who lived in the Shawano County Township of Green Valley, and lived a life very much like George; a bachelor and well enough off to not need the money. The $154,000 was put in a CD, where he took only the interest. When Mr. Gross died, as to his wishes, the inheritance money from George Putz, Jr., was split between the Shawano County Historical Society and the Shawano Area Writers. The money to the Historical Society went towards much needed repairs to the 1871 Kast Building. The funds to the Shawano Area Writers revived the six-year dormant Student Writing Contest for children in Shawano and Menominee counties. Now we are able to offer an annual $2,000 scholarship for a graduating Shawano or Menominee High School senior who wants to pursue a writing type education, especially journalism. The Student Writing Contest is now called The George Putz Memorial Student Writing Contest.

Now, I'll let you be the judge as to whether or not George Putz, Jr., was an oddball. I saw him as a man that I would hope to someday become; respected, and missed for the knowledge that was taken to the grave.

George was very concerned about whether pets go to heaven. I know he was thinking about his pet cat, Tabby. At one point, I did see an note of a Bible verse that could have indicated that animals can go to heaven.

In going through the many boxes of personal items of George's life, I uncovered something that I believe is the last thing he wrote. For most of his life George led the life of a loner, and in the end, just two months and 12 days after his beloved cat Tabby died, he began that journey himself, dying in solitude on the floor of his bedroom on May 3, 2006. He wasn't found until three days after he left this world, as we know it.

It's my belief this is the last written work of George Putz, Jr.

WhiLE WRiTiNG ThE ShAWANO PAPER MiLL CENTENNIAL BooK I HAD A HELPER, TABBY, MY LiTTLE BLACK ANO WhiTE KiTTy who SPENT MANY HoURS ON HER MAT ON MY LiBRARY TABLE AS I RECORDED ThE HiSTORY OF ThE MiLL SoMETiMES WATChiNG, SOMETiMES TAKiNG A NAP, BUT USUALLY ALWAYS ThERE. OCCASIONALLY WiTh A SWEEP OF HER TAiL ShE WOULD REARRANGE MY NOTES OR AS ShE SLEPT I WOULD HAVE To REMOVE HER TAiL OR A LEG FROM MY PAPER. I HAD HER FROM ThE TiME ShE WAS JUST OLD ENOUGh To LEAVE HER MoThER. ON FEBRUARY 15, 2006 AT 18 YEARS AND 8 MONThS ShE WENT To SLEEP FoR ThE LAST TiME. I WILL MiSS ThE LITTLE LADY.

GEORGE PUTZ JR.

About the Author

John J. Mutter, Jr., was born in the only year our country minted a steel penny. When he was five years old his parents moved to Shawano, from Racine, Wisconsin. They bought a rural grocery store/ tavern. John Sr. remodeled the back room of the tavern that was used to store beer, soda cases and empty beer barrels into a bedroom for John Jr., and his brother William.

In 1954, when the author was 11 years old he received his first writing credit for a story printed in the *Porter School Tattler*, his one-room school newspaper. In 1980, he attended the Rhinelander School of Arts for one week, taking a creative writing course, and tutored by Tere Rios Versace. Since then he has earned 153 writing credits in newspapers, newsletters, magazines, anthologies and historical journals.

He has previously published three books; was the ghostwriter for one book; wrote small biographies for several people; coordinated a book of poetry for his mother; was co-editor for the *Shawano County Sesquicentennial 1853-2003*, and through the years has received ten writing awards, along with 510 rejection letters. When John gets into a writing project, he describes himself as a, "bird-dog in knee-high grass."

John J. Mutter, Jr.
N2787 McDonald Road, Shawano, WI 54166.
Phone - 715-524-4520